Brian Abbs/Ingrid Freel

OPENING STRATEGIES
Workbook

Longman Group UK Limited
*Longman House, Burnt Mill, Harlow,
Essex CM20 2JE, England
and Associated Companies throughout the world.*

© Longman Group Limited 1984

*All rights reserved. No part of this publication
may be reproduced, stored in a retrieval system,
or transmitted in any form or by any means, electronic,
mechanical, photocopying, recording or otherwise,
without the prior written permission of the Publishers.*

First published 1984
Twentieth impression 1991

ISBN 0-582-51689-7

We are grateful to the following for permission
to reproduce copyright material:

From 'The Highway Code', reproduced with the
permission of the Controller of Her Majesty's
Stationery Office for page 57 (bottom); Longman
Photographic Unit for pages 9 and 18 (bottom);
Methodist Youth Holidays Ltd. for page 42;
Sporting Pictures (UK) Ltd. for page 27.

Designed by John Strange
Illustrated by John Fraser, Chris Ryley
and Technical Art Services.

Produced by Longman Singapore Publishers Pte Ltd.
Printed in Singapore

Contents

	page
Unit 1	2
Unit 2	7
Unit 3	12
Unit 4	19
Unit 5	25
Unit 6	28
Unit 7	33
Unit 8	38
Unit 9	44
Unit 10	50
Unit 11	53
Unit 12	57
Unit 13	61
Unit 14	67
Unit 15	71
Grammar revision	73

Unit 1

1. Match the bubbles like this:

Then write the two sentences like this:

- What's your name?
- It's 507.
- Is your name Paul?
- Good morning.
- What's her name?
- My name's Diana.
- Here's your key.
- His name's Vince.
- Are you Diana Trent?
- Thank you.
- What's your room number?
- Her name's Sally.
- What's his name?
- Yes, I am.
- Good morning.
- No it isn't. It's Jack.

1. What's your name?
   My name's Diana.
2.
3.
4.
5.
6.
7.
8.

UNIT 1

2. Write questions like this:

1. PAUL   Is his name Paul?
2. DIANA Is her name Diana?
3. VINCE ....
4. JOANNE ....
5. JACK   ....
6. SALLY ....

3. Write conversations like this:

1. YOU: Is your name Paul?
   PAUL: Yes, it is.
2. YOU: Is your name Ann?
   SALLY: No, it isn't. It's Sally.
3. YOU: .... Vince?
   VINCE: ....
4. YOU: .... Jane?
   JOANNE:................................
5. YOU: .... Sally?
   SALLY: ....
6. YOU: .... John?
   JACK: ....

UNIT 1

4. Here is the Carter family.

```
        James Carter = Ann Carter
    ┌─────────────────┼─────────────┐
Elizabeth = Carlo Pinero   Alison      David
```

Write their titles and names like this:

1. JAMES Mr J. Carter

2. ANN ....

3. ELIZABETH ....

4. ALISON ....

5. DAVID ....

6. CARLO ....

5. Complete the conversations. Write one word only in each space. Words like It's, name's, etc. count as one word.

1. A: What's *your name*?

   B: Kevin.

   A: *My name's* Jenny.

2. A: .... your name John?

   B: No, ... Mark.

3. A: .... Sally?

   B: Yes, ...

4. A: .... your key.

   B: ....

5. A: .... room number?

   B: 401.

UNIT 1

6. Write the questions like this:

1. ...What's your name?......... My name's Mark.
2. .... His name's Sandy.
3. .... Yes, it is. Mark Ellis.
4. .... No, I'm not Diana. I'm Ann.
5. .... Her name's Jane.
6. .... No, it isn't Ronald. It's Gerald.
7. .... 14, King Street, Bournemouth
8. .... 805 9866
9. .... Room 202

7. Write Good morning, Good afternoon or Good evening in the bubbles.

UNIT 1

8. Write the answers like this:

4+6= *ten*

1. 5+2= ....
2. 2+1+5= ....
3. 10−7= ....
4. 9−5+1= ....
5. 8−7= ....
6. 8−2= ....
7. 6+7−11= ....
8. 3×3= ....
9. 4×2−4= ....
10. 15−5= ....

9. Crossword

Across

3. 2+3= ....
4. Good ....
6. Please write .... phone.
8. 5×2= ....
9. What's .... name?
10. Is .... name Ann?
13. What's your .... number?
14. Is .... name Paul?
16. My ....'s Diana.
18. Good morning .... Roberts.

Down

1. Good ....
2. A: Here's your key.
   B: ....
5. A: Are you Sally?
   B: ...., I'm not.
7. 7−4= ....
11. Diana and Paul are at the Tower ....
12. Your room number is 201. Here's your ....
15. My .... number is 407.
17. Diana is in room 201 .... Paul is in room 202.

Unit 2

1. Which is correct, a, b or c?

1. A: Hello. B: (a) Hello. Pleased to meet you.
   b) How do you do.
   c) Good morning.

2. A: How do you do. B: a) Good, thank you.
   b) How do you do.
   c) Good evening.

3. A: This is Joanne. B: a) Goodbye, Joanne.
   b) Thank you, Joanne.
   c) Hi. Pleased to meet you, Joanne.

4. A: Where are you from? B: a) Italian.
   b) From Italy.
   c) In Italy.

5. A: Are you two English? B: a) No, we aren't.
   b) No, I'm not.
   c) No, you aren't.

6. A: Are they from the States? B: a) Yes, it is.
   b) Yes, they're here.
   c) Yes, they are.

2. Write the nationalities of the following people:

1. Sasha is from Japan. *She's Japanese.*
2. Hank is from the States. *He's American.*
3. Jean-Michel is from France. ....
4. Diana is from Britain. ....
5. Oumon is from Senegal. ....
6. Ramon is from Spain. ....
7. Claudia is from Italy. ....
8. Antonieta is from Brazil. ....
9. Karl is from Germany. ....
10. Aristotle is from Greece. ....

UNIT 2

3. Write sentences about people's nationalities, like this:

1. They/Italian/Spanish — They aren't Italian. They're Spanish.
2. We/English/American ......
3. She/Japanese/Chinese ......
4. He/Spanish/Brazilian ......
5. We/Italian/French ......
6. They/American/British ......
7. She/Danish/Swedish ......
8. I/American/Canadian ......

4. What's this in English? Write the answers.

1. pam
2. eky
3. serddas obok
4. bomc
5. elalbrum
6. awellt
7. ryida
8. seurp

1. It's a map.
2. ......
3. ......
4. ......
5. ......
6. ......
7. ......

5. Write as you speak. Write the short forms of the sentences like this:

1. I am English. — I'm English.
2. He is Spanish. ......
3. She is not American. ......
4. We are from the States. ......
5. It is Japanese. ......
6. They are not Italian. ......
7. It is not very good. ......
8. They are nice. ......

6. Punctuate these sentences with full stops (.) and capital letters where necessary.

jenny richards is an english teacher at the tower language school she is from london she is a very good teacher

....

....

....

....

....

The Tower Language School
Students' Union Membership

Name: Michelle Duprès
Address: 29, Addison Road, London, W.8
Tel: 943 1061
Place of birth: Chartres, France

The Tower Language School
Students' Union Membership

Name: Ricardo Vargas
Address: 4, Woodville Avenue, London, S.E.9
Tel: 727 9980
Place of birth: São Paulo, Brazil

7. Write he's, his, she's or her in the sentences.

1. **She's** French.

2. .... first name is Michelle.

3. .... address in England is 29, Addison Road, London, W.8.

4. .... Brazilian.

5. .... surname is Vargas.

6. .... telephone number is 943 1061.

7. .... from São Paulo.

8. .... from Chartres in France.

9. .... address in London is 4, Woodville Avenue, London, S.E.9.

10. .... surname is Duprès.

8. Complete the conversation with words from this box:

are	'm	's	meet	this
're	am	is	telephone	there
aren't		isn't	from	here's

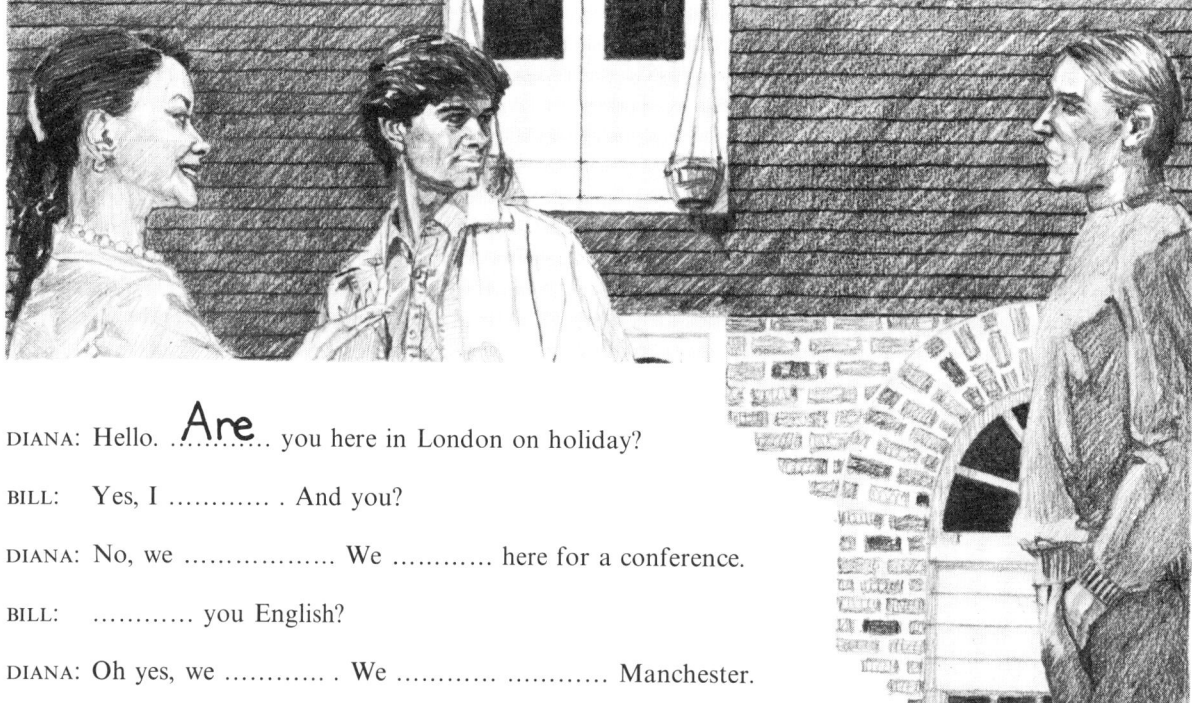

DIANA: Hello. ..Are.. you here in London on holiday?

BILL: Yes, I .... And you?

DIANA: No, we .... We .... here for a conference.

BILL: .... you English?

DIANA: Oh yes, we .... We .... Manchester.
I .... Diana and .... is Paul.

BILL: Hello. Pleased to .... you.

PAUL: Hello.

BILL: What .... the name of your hotel?

DIANA: The Tower Hotel. It .... over ....

BILL: .... your hotel good?

PAUL: Yes, it .... near the river.

BILL: That's nice. What .... the .... number?

DIANA: It's 481 2575. but .... their card.

BILL: Thanks. I'll phone for a room there, I think.

UNIT 2

9. Write the questions like this:

1. *Where are you from?* — From Japan.
2. .... — No, I'm not British. I'm American.
3. .... — Her address is 29, Addison Road.
4. .... — We're from the States.
5. .... — That's right. American.

10. Picture crossword

Across

Down

Unit 3

1. Use the information about Sandra and Brian to complete the dialogue below.

Sandra Walker	Brian Walker
Likes: pop music cats	Likes: classical music dogs

MAN: Hello. *What's your name?*

SANDRA: My name's Sandra Walker.

MAN: And ....?

SANDRA: My brother's name is Brian.

MAN: .... both like pop music?

SANDRA: Well, I do, but Brian .... He .... classical music.

MAN: What about animals?

SANDRA: I ...., but Brian ....

He .... like cats at all.

MAN: So you and your brother don't like the same things.

SANDRA: No, we ....

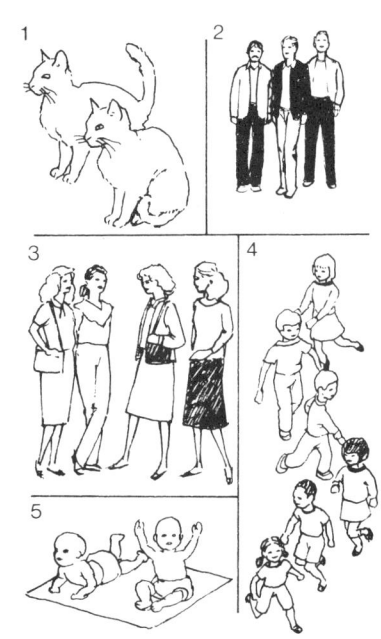

2. Write what you see in the pictures.

1. *Two cats* ....
2. ....
3. ....
4. ....
5. ....

UNIT 3

3. Punctuate these sentences with capital letters, full stops and apostrophes (') where necessary.

my names joan and im a computer programmer i work for a computer company called icl my boss is called mr blake hes very nice im mr blakes assistant

....

....

....

....

4. Put the words in the right order. Start each sentence with a capital letter.

1. job much I like very don't my.   *I don't like my job very much.*
2. doesn't like hotel his he.   ....
3. room they like don't hotel the.   ....
4. like do this you coffee?   ....
5. this place a is nice.   ....
6. there Paul that's over.   ....

5. Fill in the missing letters of the words below and match the jobs with the right people.

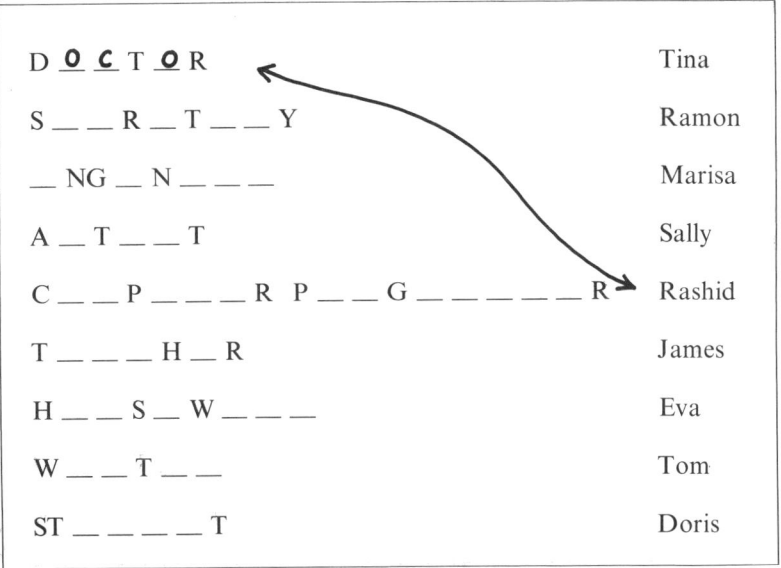

D <u>O</u> C T <u>O</u> R	Tina
S _ _ R _ T _ _ Y	Ramon
_ NG _ N _ _ _ _	Marisa
A _ T _ _ T	Sally
C _ P _ _ _ R P _ _ G _ _ _ _ _ R	Rashid
T _ _ _ H _ R	James
H _ _ S _ W _ _ _	Eva
W _ _ T _ _	Tom
ST _ _ _ _ _ T	Doris

13

UNIT 3

Write sentences about each person, like this:

1. Rashid is a doctor.
2. ....
3. ....
4. ....
5. ....
6. ....
7. ....
8. ....
9. ....

6. Look at the pictures of the people in Exercise 5 and complete these dialogues.

1. What's your name?
   My name's Eva.
   What do you do, Eva?
   I'm a computer programmer.

2. What's your name?
   ....
   What do you do, Rashid?
   ....

3. What's your name?
   ....
   What do you do, Sally?
   ....

4. What's your name?
   ....
   What do you do, Tina?
   ....

5. What's your name?
   ....
   What do you do, Tom?
   ....

UNIT 3

7. Complete this dialogue.

GIRL: Meet my friend, John Ritchie.

YOU: How do you do. My name's ....

JOHN: How do you do.

YOU: .... John?

JOHN: I'm an artist. And what ....?

YOU: ....

JOHN: Oh really? This is my wife, Anna.

ANNA: ....

YOU: How do you do.

JOHN: Anna .... a computer company.

YOU: ....

ANNA: We live in Solihull near Birmingham.

8. Write questions and answers.

1. Tina/engineer (✓)
   Is Tina an engineer?
   Yes, she is.
2. Rashid/teacher (×)
   Is Rashid a teacher?
   No, he isn't. He's a doctor.
3. Sally/computer programmer (×)

   ....

   ....
4. Ramon/teacher (✓)

   ....

   ....
5. Marisa/artist (×)

   ....

   ....

15

UNIT 3

6. James/student (×)

   ....

   ....

7. Tom/waiter (✓)

   ....

   ....

8. Georgie/dental nurse (✓)

   ....

   ....

9. Complete this dialogue.

Angela Laucas is at the Tower Language School.

ANGELA: Good morning.

SECRETARY: *Good morning.* ....

ANGELA: I want to come to English classes here.

SECRETARY: That's fine. .... , please?

ANGELA: Laucas.

SECRETARY: ....

ANGELA: L-A-U-C-A-S.

SECRETARY: Thank you. And ....

ANGELA: From Recife in Brazil.

SECRETARY: .... ?

ANGELA: .... receptionist for Varig Airlines.

UNIT 3

10. Put in the right word.
Choose from the words in the box.

| with | by | in | for | from | of |

1. He's called Dave ...**by**... his friends.

2. I live .... the south .... France.

3. She works .... a company called ICL.

4. They're American. They're .... Los Angeles. Los Angeles is .... California.

5. He's married .... three children. His wife, Kathleen, is .... Belfast in Ireland.

11. Write dialogues.

1. you/north of England/south of Lancaster

A: *Where do you live?*
B: *I live in the north of England.*
A: *Really? Where exactly?*
B: *South of Lancaster.*

2. they/south of England/north of Bournemouth

A: ....
B: ....
A: ....
B: ....

3. she/west of England/north-east of Exeter

A: ....
B: ....
A: ....
B: ....

UNIT 3

12. Read and fill in the gaps below.
Use a, an, the, in, for, from, of.

Jack Matthews is ...an... engineer on .... cruise ship called .... QE2. He works .... company called Cunard. It's .... big British shipping company. Jack lives .... Southampton, ... big city .... south .... England, but in fact he is .... Bangor, ... town .... North Wales.

13. Use the form to write about Helen Baker.

NAME:	Helen Mary Baker
MARITAL STATUS:	Married
CHILDREN:	2
NATIONALITY:	British
PLACE OF BIRTH:	Newcastle upon Tyne
OCCUPATION:	Doctor's receptionist
ADDRESS:	4, Freeman Road, Newcastle upon Tyne

Start like this: Helen Baker is British and comes from

Unit 4

1. Find the food and drink words in the puzzle. Some letters are used more than once. There are 10 words altogether. Write them like this:

1. milk
2. ....
3. ....
4. ....
5. ....
6. ....
7. ....
8. ....
9. ....
10. ....

```
A R M I L K W Z F N
R G C H E G G D C F
I J O K V L M B H N
B O C C O F F E E B
I H A D N Q O E E R
S S C T R U R D S F
C H O C O L A T E Y
U O L A Q V N W X Z
I M A K O L G T O N
T E A E I B E M P A
```

2. Look at the words in the box below and put them under the right picture.

| cake | coffee | biscuits | orange juice | tea | milk |
| bread | cheese | sweets | Coca-cola | peanuts | water |

a cup of

coffee
....
....
....
....

a glass of
....
....
....
....
....

a piece of
....
....
....
....
....

a packet of
....
....
....
....
....

Now choose one word from each group and put it in a sentence like this:

1. Can I have a cup of coffee, please?
2. .... glass ....
3. .... piece ....
4. .... packet ....

UNIT 4

3. Paul and Joanne are in a café.

PAUL: Do you want a cup of coffee?
JOANNE: Yes, please.
PAUL: And a sandwich?
JOANNE: No, thanks. Just a cup of coffee.

PAUL: Two cups of coffee, please.

PAUL: Here you are. Here's your coffee.
JOANNE: Thanks.

Now you write the words in the bubbles below. Ask if Joanne wants a cup of tea and a piece of cake.

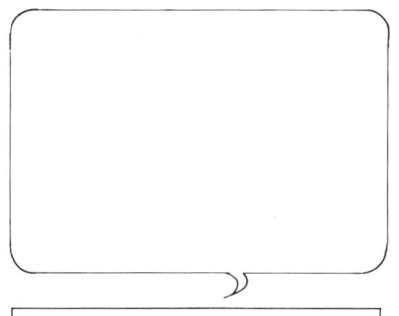  

UNIT 4

4. Write dialogues using this or these. Write about the objects in the pictures below.

1. A: How much is this comb?
   B: It's forty-five pence.
2. A: How much are these pens?
   B: They're seventy-five pence.
3. A: ....
   B: ....
4. A: ....
   B: ....
5. A: ....
   B: ....
6. A: ....
   B: ....

5. Look at the objects in Exercise 4. Say you like them, using that or those, and ask the price. Write sentences like this:

1. I like that comb. How much is it?
2. I like those pens. How much are they?
3. ....
4. ....
5. ....
6. ....

UNIT 4

6. Write the next numbers in the sequence.

1. TWO   FOUR   SIX   EIGHT   ......TEN......   ......TWELVE......   ......FOURTEEN......
2. ONE   THREE   FIVE   SEVEN   NINE   ....
3. FIVE   TEN   FIFTEEN   ....
4. TEN   TWENTY   THIRTY   ....
5. TWO   FOUR   EIGHT   SIXTEEN   ....
6. ZERO   TEN   HUNDRED   ....

7. Write dialogues. Use the words in brackets like this:

1. (I/swim)   A: *I like swimming.*
   B: *Really?*
   A: *Yes, I swim a lot.*

2. (He/ski)   A: ....
   B: ....
   A: ....

3. (They/go to the theatre)   A: ....
   B: ....
   A: ....

4. (She/read)   A: ....
   B: ....
   A: ....

5. (We/watch television)   A: ....
   B: ....
   A: ....

6. (They/play video games)   A: ....
   B: ....
   A: ....

UNIT 4

8. Complete the requests.

1. I like John Travolta. Can I have a photograph of ......him...... ?
2. I like Olivia Newton-John. Can I have a photograph of .... ?
3. I like the Rolling Stones. Can I have a photograph of .... ?
4. I love the Muppets. Can I have a photograph of .... ?
5. I like you a lot. Can I have a photograph of .... ?

9. Complete the conversation between Rita and Roger. Use the information in the table.

Name:	Rita
Likes:	Chocolate cake, Coca-cola, sitting in cafés
Dislikes:	tea, tomato sandwiches, watching television, going to discos

Name:	Roger
Likes:	Chocolate cake, tea
Dislikes:	Coca-cola, tomato sandwiches, watching television, sitting in cafés, going to discos

RITA: I like chocolate cake.
ROGER: Yes, so do I.
RITA: I don't like tea.
ROGER: Don't you? I do.
RITA: I don't like going to discos.
ROGER: No, nor do I.
RITA: .... Coca-cola.
ROGER: ....
RITA: .... tomato sandwiches.
ROGER: ....
RITA: .... sitting in cafés.
ROGER: ....
RITA: .... watching television.
ROGER: ....

UNIT 4

10. You want to interview a friend for your class magazine. Use the headings below to write the questions for the interview.

QUESTIONNAIRE

Name: *What's your name?*

Nationality: *Where are you from?*

Job: ....

Interests: ....

Entertainment

   cinema: *Do you like going to the cinema?*

   theatre: ....

   parties: ....

   television: ....

Sports

   swimming: ....

   tennis: ....

   football: ....

Languages: ....

....

Now interview your friend. Note down the answers and write a paragraph or two about your friend in your notebook.

Start like this: *My friend's name is*

Unit 5 | Consolidation

1. Fill in the correct question words. Choose from:

> Who? What? Where? How? How much? How old?

1. A: .... are you from?   B: From Ireland.
2. A: .... is that ham sandwich?   B: It's 35 pence.
3. A: .... are you?   B: I'm fine, thanks.
4. A: .... do you do.   B: How do you do.
5. A: .... are you?   B: I'm nineteen.
6. A: .... are you?   B: I'm the manager here.
7. A: .... is your mother called?   B: Mabel.
8. A: .... do you do?   B: I'm a student.
9. A: .... is Birmingham?   B: It's in the middle of England.
10. A: .... sort of music do you like?   B: I like modern jazz and reggae.

2. Punctuate this part of a letter. Put capital letters, apostrophes, full stops and question marks where necessary.

dear john
    how are you im fine thanks for your letter i like reading your letters theyre great fun thanks also for your brothers address how are tinas children please write and tell me all about them

UNIT 5

3. Look at these prices of rooms in the Tower Hotel.

Write questions and answers about the prices of rooms, like this:

1. A: How much is a single room?
   B: It's £48 per night.

2. A: .... the double rooms?
   B: ....

3. A: .... a twin room with an extra bed?
   B: ....

4. A: .... a studio single for two nights?
   B: ....

5. A: .... the penthouse suites?
   B: ....

4.

Focus on Paul Goddard
WEST HAM

FULL NAME: Paul Goddard

BIRTHPLACE: Hayes, Middlesex

BIRTH DATE: October 12, 1959

MARRIED: To Debbie

CHILDREN: None

CAR: Fiat X1/9

FAVOURITE NEWSPAPER: *Daily Mail*

FAVOURITE OTHER SPORT: I enjoy all sports

FAVOURITE FOOD AND DRINK: Scampi and milk

FAVOURITE HOLIDAY RESORT: Barbados

FAVOURITE SINGERS: Olivia Newton-John, Stevie Wonder

LIKES: playing golf, playing with my dog, going to discos with my friends

DISLIKES: washing up and rainy days

Write six facts about Paul in your notebook like this:

Paul Goddard is a footballer from Hayes, Middlesex.
He plays football for West Ham.

Unit 6

1. Fill in the missing verbs. Choose from the verbs in the box.

| am ('m) | was | is ('s) | are | were |
| am not ('m not) | wasn't | isn't | aren't | weren't |

DIANA: Hello, Vince.

VINCE: Hi! How ..**are**.. you?

DIANA: I .... fine. And you?

VINCE: I .... very well.

DIANA: Oh! Really? I'm sorry.

VINCE: Yes. I .... at the conference today. I .... in bed.

DIANA: Well, don't worry. It .... very interesting.

VINCE: .... you and Paul both there?

DIANA: No, we .... Paul .... at a meeting with EMI.

Where .... Joanne now?

VINCE: I don't know. She .... here at lunchtime. By the way, Diana, ... those Japanese people from JVC?

DIANA: No, they .... I asked them. They .... from Sony.

VINCE: Ah! That .... interesting. Thank you.

2. Write conversations.

1. A: Where/you last night?

   B: We/at home.

   A: Where were you last night?

   B: We were at home.

2. A: The party/fun?

   B: Yes/quite fun.

   A: Was the party fun?

   B: Yes, it was quite fun.

3. A: Where/your teacher last week?

   B: She/on holiday.

   A: ....

   B: ....

UNIT 6

4. A: The lecture/interesting?   A: ....
   B: Yes/very interesting.   B: ....

5. A: You/meeting this morning? A: ....
   B: No/in bed.   B: ....

6. A: They/conference yesterday afternoon?   A: ....
   B: Yes/there all day.   B: ....

3. Answer these questions.

Where were you at 6 o'clock this morning? ....

at 9 o'clock last night? ....

this time last week? ....

yesterday morning? ....

4. Give directions. Start from the point marked X on the map and direct people to:

1. the cinema *Turn left at the café and the cinema is on your right.*

2. the shoe shop ....

3. the record shop ....

4. the book shop ....

5. the chemist's ....

UNIT 6

5. Write these times.

1. 6 a.m. ...Six in the morning...
2. 4 a.m. ....
3. 7 p.m. ....
4. 8 p.m. ....
5. 2 p.m. ....
6. 10 a.m. ....

6. Answer these questions.

1. When does the train leave? (13.45) ...It leaves at quarter to two.
2. does it arrive? (14.30) ....
3. does the film start? (19.45) ....
4. does *Match of the Day* start? (15.00) ....
5. does your flight leave? (21.05) ....
6. does Harrods close? (18.00) ....

7. Write conversations.

1. film – start 7 p.m. – finish 9 p.m.

A: ...What time does the film start?
B: ...At seven.
A: ...And what time does it finish?
B: ...At nine.

2. bus – leave 6.10 a.m. – arrive 6.50 a.m.

A: ....
B: ....
A: ....
B: ....

3. book shop – open 10 a.m. – close 6 p.m.

A: ....
B: ....
A: ....
B: ....

UNIT 6

Tourist Information Board   April 10th–17th

Welcome to Brentham-on-Sea

BANKS:	Midland	12, Hertford Street	hours 9.30 a.m.–3.30 p.m.
	Lloyds	10, High Street	hours 9.30 a.m.–3.30 p.m.
POST OFFICE:		14, High Street	hours 9.00 a.m.–5.30 p.m.
DEPARTMENT STORES:			
	A & N	46, Hertford Street	hours 9.00 a.m.–6.00 p.m.
			early closing Wednesday 1.00 p.m.
	Bailey's	21, Downes Street	hours 9.30 a.m.–6.00 p.m.
			late night Thursday 7.00 p.m.

CINEMAS:			
	The Odeon	High Street	*The Return of the Jedi* (AA)
			Progs. 1.30 4.45 8.05
	Cinecenta	Hertford Street	*E.T. The Extra Terrestrial* (AA)
			Progs. 2.00 5.35 9.10

8. Write the questions for these answers.

1. A: *What time does the post office close?*

   B: At 5.30 p.m.

2. A: .... on Wednesday?

   B: At 1.00 p.m.

3. A: .... on Thursday?

   B: At 7.00 p.m.

4. A: ....

   B: In Downes Street.

5. A: ....

   B: There are two. The Odeon and the Cinecenta.

6. A: ....

   B: They open at 9.30 a.m.

7. A: ....

   B: At 2.00 p.m.

UNIT 6

9. Punctuate this letter. Put in commas, apostrophes, full stops, capital letters and question marks where necessary. Write the letter in your notebook.

dear simon
how are you hows sam were you at the martins last night i telephoned you but you werent in was the lunch at the whites fun im very well but i miss you
write soon
lots of love
carol

10. Crossword

Across

4. A: What's the time?
   B: It's six ....
7. You and I
8. Not last
10. 6+4= ....
11. What's .... at the cinema?
12. Also
13. Can I play a ....?
16. Not she
17. The shop .... at nine in the morning.
20. He isn't at work, he's at ....
21. The match .... at three o'clock.
25. Three o'clock .... the morning.
26. Scandinavian Airline Services.
27. He's not well. He's in ....
28. Is .... a bank near here?

Down

1. The .... office closes at 5.30 p.m.
2. All right
3. Not him
5. Not early
6. A: Can you ski?
   B: No, I ....
7. A drink
8. He works .... the BBC.
9. Is there a .... shop near here?
14. You can buy a film here.
15. What time .... the bank close?
18. A: I don't like dogs.
    B: .... do I.
19. .... is Henry. He's a student here.
22. What .... is it? Ten o'clock?
23. He's .... air steward.
24. A: Do you like the Smiths?
    B: Yes, I like .... very much.

Unit 7

1. Which is correct, a, b or c?

1. What time do you get up?
   - a) At half past seven. ✓
   - b) At thirty past seven.
   - c) At seven and a half.

2. What time does he get up?
   - a) He's get up at six.
   - b) He get up at six.
   - c) He gets up at six.

3. a) When he starts work?
   b) When does he start work?
   c) When does he starts work?

   At half past nine.

4. What are they doing?
   - a) They do exercises.
   - b) They're doing exercises.
   - c) There doing exercises.

5. I get up late
   - a) on Sundays.
   - b) every Sundays.
   - c) in Sunday.

6. I go to yoga classes
   - a) in Monday evenings.
   - b) every Monday evening.
   - c) on the evening of Monday.

7. a) What's the weather like?
   b) What the weather is like?
   c) What does the weather like?

   It's beautiful.

8. a) Isn't it an awful weather!
   b) Isn't it an awful day!
   c) Isn't it awful day?

   Yes, it's terrible.

2. Join both halves and make sensible sentences.

1. He gets up
2. They usually go out for a beer
3. The weather is awful
4. They have lunch
5. He's living in London
6. He stays in bed

in the canteen.
now.
late on Sundays.
at seven in the morning.
in Scotland in winter.
after supper.

1. *He gets up at seven in the morning.*
2.
3.
4.
5.
6.

UNIT 7

3. Complete the conversation.

A: Isn't it a lovely day!

B: Yes, ... great!

A: I love .... across the park. .... so much to see.

B: Yes, look .... that girl! .... is she standing on her head?

A: .... Let's ask her.

Er .... me! Why .... ?

C: .... yoga. I .... yoga every day in the park.

A: Goodness! I don't .... any exercise.

4. Find the missing words. Choose from the box:

11 p.m.	he likes cooking	in the canteen
architect	Manchester	a cup of coffee and an egg
7.30 a.m.	after work	at 8.30 a.m.
watching TV and reading the paper		

Simon Trent lives in .... (1).

He's an .... (2).

Every morning he gets up up at .... (3).

He has .... (4).

for breakfast and leaves the house .... (5).

He usually has lunch .... (6) at work.

He does the shopping .... (7)

and makes supper for his wife and daughter in the evening

because .... (8).

After supper he likes ....

.... (9). He goes to bed at .... (10).

UNIT 7

Now write the question for each numbered statement.

1. Where *does Simon Trent live?*
2. What ....
3. When ....
4. What ....
5. What time ....
6. Where ....
7. When ....
8. Why ....
9. What ....
10. When ....

5. Complete the sentences as you like, using a negative.

1. I speak English, but I *don't speak German.*
2. He likes tea, but he ....
3. I can skate, but I ....
4. She likes cooking, but she ....
5. He plays football, but he ....
6. They get up early, but they ....
7. She goes to bed late on Saturdays, but ....

6. Write about your own routines. Use the words in brackets.

1. (every day) *I get up at half past seven every day.*
2. (on Sundays) ....
3. (on Friday evenings) ....
4. (every morning) ....
5. (every evening) ....
6. (at the weekend) ....
7. (on Saturdays) ....

UNIT 7

7. Write this letter. Use the correct form of the verb in brackets.

> Dear Robert,
> I (write) this in the lounge of the Grand Hotel. We (stay) here for our holiday because it is so near the centre. The kids (enjoy) every minute of it. Sarah (shop) just now and (buy) all her Christmas presents – already!
> See you soon,
> Love,
> Jill

8. Reorder these letters and spell the days of the week.

DYNEWESAD	YADNOM	UASTYED
YUNASD	IFAYRD	ASTYDRUA
SUTDHRYA		

Answer these questions.

1. What day is it today? ....

2. What day is it tomorrow? ....

3. What day was it yesterday? ....

4. What day of the week is your birthday this year? ....

UNIT 7

9. Here is the Ewing family tree:

```
                    Jock = Ellie
      ┌──────────────┬──────┴──────┬──────────────┐
   J.R. = Sue Ellen  Ray = Donna  Bobby = Pamela  Gary = Valerie
      │                                                │
   John Ross                                         Lucy
```

Write sentences about these relations:

1. J.R./Sue Ellen ...He's her husband...
2. J.R./Ellie ....
3. Ellie/J.R., Ray, Bobby and Gary ....
   ....
4. Jock and Ellie/Lucy ....
   ....
5. John Ross/Jock ....
   ....
6. Pamela/Bobby ....
7. Gary/J.R. ....
8. Lucy/Gary ....

10. World weather. Make conversations about the weather in each place.

1. A: What's the weather like in Copenhagen?
   B: It's snowing and very cold.
2. A: .... Alexandria?
   B: It's fine and quite hot.
3. A: .... Amsterdam?
   B: ....
4. A: .... Barbados?
   B: ....
5. A: .... Moscow?
   B: ....
6. A: .... Glasgow?
   B: ....

World weather

		°C
Alexandria	F	26
Amsterdam	C	11
Barbados	S	30
Copenhagen	Sn	−1
Glasgow	R	10
Moscow	Sn	−5

F= Fine
C= Cloudy
S= Sunny
R= Rain
Sn= Snow

Unit 8

1. A journalist is interviewing some people about their journeys to work. Fill in the questions.

JOURNALIST: Excuse me. I'm doing an article about how people travel to work. Can you answer some questions?

MAN: Yes, of course.

JOURNALIST: My first question is, how do ....

MAN: Oh, I usually go by tube.

JOURNALIST: ....

MAN: Cycle? No, never. I haven't got a bicycle.

JOURNALIST: ....

MAN: It's about 5 miles.

JOURNALIST: ....

MAN: About 20 minutes.

JOURNALIST: Right. Thank you very much.

2. This graph shows how people travel to work in Helsinki. Two hundred people were interviewed.

Write five sentences like this:

1. *Out of 200 people, 40% cycle to work.*
2. ....
3. ....
4. ....
5. ....

And two sentences starting like this:

6. In Helsinki, most people ....
....

7. Only a few ....

UNIT 8

3. Write the names of the rooms and places in a hotel on the pictures.

 1
 2
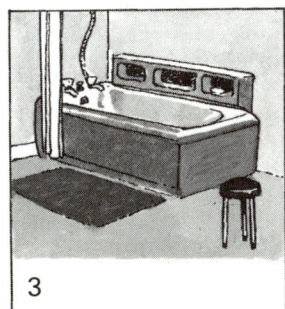 3
 4
 5
 6
 7

4. Write in How many, How much, How far, How long **or** How often.

1. **How much** is a cup of coffee?
2. .... bedrooms have you got?
3. .... does it take you to get to work?
4. .... do you go swimming?
5. .... was the meal at that Italian restaurant?
6. .... is it from here to Manchester?
7. .... miles is it to London?
8. .... do you see your parents?
9. .... did it take you to get here?
10. .... is the sea from here?

UNIT 8

5. Circle the word which is different in each group.

A	B	C	D	E	F
bedroom	walk	sometimes	how	green	drives
(garden)	bus	usually	who	red	walk
kitchen	car	now	where	coffee	cycles
bathroom	train	often	there	yellow	goes

6. Look at the floor plan of this hotel.

Where's the restaurant?	It's on the ground/first/second/top floor. next to the women's toilets. opposite the lift.

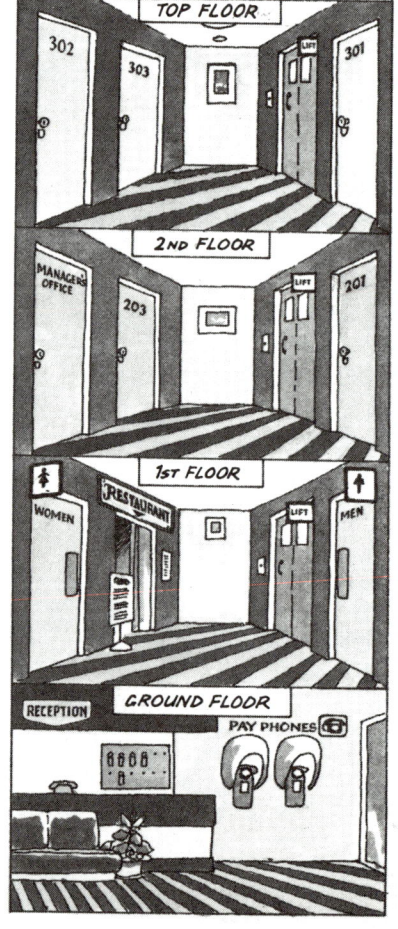

Ask and answer:

1. A: Where's Room 303?
   B: It's on the top floor, opposite the lift.

2. A: .... the manager's office?
   B: ....
   ....

3. A: .... the women's toilets?
   B: ....
   ....

4. A: .... the telephones?
   B: ....
   ....

5. A: .... the men's toilets?
   B: ....
   ....

UNIT 8

7. Fill in the missing words. Choose from the words in the box.

lives	work	at	a	sometimes
visits	doesn't	in	an	only
walks	but	on	he	late
comes				

Derek Matthews ...**comes**... from Reading but he .... live there now. He .... in London. He is .... teacher in a school .... North London. He usually .... to school but he .... cycles when he is .... It takes about half .... hour to walk but .... ten minutes to cycle. .... has got a car .... he never drives to .... He drives the car .... the weekend. He often .... his parents in Reading .... Saturday or Sunday.

8. Make conversations like this:

1. tea/coffee/chocolate

   A: What would you like?
   B: What is there?
   A: There's tea, coffee or chocolate
   B: I'd like coffee, please.

2. beef/chicken/lamb

   A: ....
   B: ....
   A: ....
   B: ....

3. ice cream/apple pie/fruit salad

   A: ....
   B: ....
   A: ....
   B: ....

UNIT 8

9. Now make conversations like this:

1. tea/cake

   A: Would you like some more tea?
   B: Yes, please. I'd love some.
   A: What about some more cake?
   B: No, thanks. That's fine.

2. wine/cheese

   A: ....
   B: ....
   A: ....
   B: ....

3. apple pie/cream

   A: ....
   B: ....
   A: ....
   B: ....

10. You are a teacher and you want to take a group of young people to England for a study holiday. You see this advertisement in a newspaper.

Planning your 1984
SCHOOL JOURNEY?

A welcome awaits you at the unique

**MUNDESLEY YOUTH
HOLIDAY CENTRE**

Accommodation in Dormitories, Bedrooms or Camping in campus of over 6 acres very near the sea, countryside and the Norfolk Broads.

Write or phone for details and colour brochure:-

METHODIST YOUTH HOLIDAYS LTD. (T),
Paston Road, Mundesley, Norfolk NR11 8BN.
Tel: (0263) 720325

UNIT 8

You want some more information. You decide to ring the Centre. Write questions to get the following information. These questions will help you:

> How many .... are there?
> Is there a ....?
> How much/How long/How far ....?

1. Number of bedrooms? ...How many bedrooms are there?...
2. Number of toilets on each floor? ....
3. Colour TV? ....
4. Table tennis table? ....
5. Swimming pool? ....
6. Far from the sea? ....
7. How long by train from London? ....
8. Cost for 24 students for 7 days? ....

11. Use information on the right to write the warden's answers to your questions.

1. ...There are fifteen bedrooms (with four beds in each room)...
2. ....
3. ....
4. ....
5. ....
6. ....
7. ....
8. ....

MUNDESLEY YOUTH HOLIDAY CENTRE

This beautiful country house is on four floors and can accommodate up to 60 people. Each upstairs floor has five dormitories (bedrooms) each with four beds. On each floor there are two bathrooms and two toilets which the guests share. On the ground floor, there is a dining room, a large recreation room for games including table tennis and a colour TV. There is also a sauna in the basement. The hotel is situated about five minutes from the sea. Connections with London are good: a fast Inter-City train taking under two hours. Group bookings accepted at the Centre: cost £50 per person per week.
Warden: Mr. C. Haddon

43

Unit 9

1. Which is right, a, b or c?

1. Hello! Is that Judy?
   a) Yes, she is speaking.
   b) Yes, I am speaking.
   c) Yes, speaking. ✓

2. a) Is there anything interesting to see?
   b) Is there anything of interesting to see?
   c) Is there anything is interesting to see?

3. a) Can I speak to Jill please?
   b) Can I speak Jill please?
   c) Please, I want to speak to Jill.

4. Shall we go out?
   a) Yes, we shall.
   b) Yes, let's.
   c) Yes, we will.

5. a) Do you enjoy the film last night?
   b) Did you enjoyed the film last night?
   c) Did you enjoy the film last night?

6. a) Hello! I am Diana speaking.
   b) Hello! It's Diana here.
   c) Hello! She's Diana here.

7. Would you like to go out?
   a) Yes, I'd love to.
   b) Yes, I like to.
   c) Yes, I love to.

8. Are you free
   a) on May the 18th?
   b) in May the 18th?
   c) at May the 18th?

2. Put the conversation in the right order.

A: ...e)...
B: ....
A: ....
B: ....
A: ....
B: ....
A: ....
B: ....
A: ....
B: ....
A: ....
B: ....

a) Jane! How are you?
b) How nice! Yes, I'd love to. Where is it on?
c) Hello. Can I speak to Sue, please?
d) I've got two tickets for Handel's *Messiah*. Would you like to come with me?
e) 9876. Hello.
f) January the 23rd. Er . . . Yes, I am. Why?
g) Sue, it's Jane here.
h) Yes, fine! See you there. Bye! And thanks, Jane.
i) Oh, not too bad. Listen, are you free on January the 23rd?
j) At the Festival Hall. Shall we meet outside at about 7.15?
k) That's OK. See you on the 23rd then. Bye!
l) Speaking. Who is it?

UNIT 9

3. Put the words in the right order. Start each sentence with a capital letter.

1. last you the enjoy party did night?
   ....

2. like very parties much to doesn't going Jane.
   ....

3. London to take it how to does long get?
   ....

4. third on bedroom is our floor the.
   ....

**4. This is how a race finished. Which horse won?
Which colour came first, which came second, and so on?**

1st Red came first.
2nd ....
3rd ....
4th ....
5th ....

5. Write the dates.

1. 3.3.81 3rd March 1981
2. 1.5.46 ....
3. 30.10.83 ....
4. 25.12.82 ....
5. 17.7.56 ....
6. 21.1.75 ....

UNIT 9

6. Use the diary to make conversations. Use in the morning, in the afternoon, in the evening.

JUNE

Monday 21st	Tuesday 22nd	Wednesday 23rd	Thursday
a.m.	a.m. Dentist 11 a.m.	a.m. Computer course	a.m.
p.m. Meeting at school 3.30–4.30 p.m.	p.m. Dinner at Samson's 8 p.m.	p.m.	p.m.
Friday 25th	Saturday 26th a.m.	Sunday 27th a.m.	Note

1. A: Are you free on Monday the 21st in the morning?
   B: Yes, I am.

2. A: Are you free on Monday the 21st in the afternoon?
   B: No, I'm afraid I'm not.

3. A:
   B:

4. A:
   B:

5. A:
   B:

6. A:
   B:

7. A:
   B:

8. A:
   B:

UNIT 9

7. Make conversations like this:

1. film (✓)

   A: How was the film?
   B: I liked it very much.

2. programme (✗) (long)

   A: How was the programme?
   B: I didn't like it very much. It was too long.

3. play (✓)

   A: ....
   B: ....

4. sightseeing trip (✗) (slow)

   A: ....
   B: ....

5. holiday in Spain (✗) (hot)

   A: ....
   B: ....

6. meal (✓)

   A: ....
   B: ....

7. film (✗) (sad)

   A: ....
   B: ....

8. a rock concert (✗) (loud)

   A: ....
   B: ....

9. a fancy dress party (✓)

   A: ....
   B: ....

UNIT 9

8. What children think

(A Strategies survey of some children's opinions)

Strategies took four children – Jessica, Sushi, William and Ben – from Class 2 of Montpelier Primary School to the Junior National Film Theatre. They saw a different film every Saturday for 4 weeks. These are their opinions.

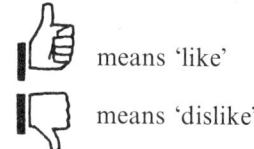

👍 means 'like'

👎 means 'dislike'

Title of film	Jessica	Sushi	William	Ben
1. THE SOUND OF MUSIC	👍 'It was lovely.'	👍 'It was super.'	👎 'It was too slow.'	👍 'It was nice.'
2. THE WIZARD OF OZ	👎 'It was too sad'	👍 'It was frightening, but good.'	👍 'It was good.'	👍 'It was all right.'
3. STAR WARS	👎 'It was too noisy.'	👎 'It was too frightening.'	👍 'It was fantastic.'	👍 'It was great.'
4. The Black Stallion	👍 'It was beautiful.'	👍 'I like horses.'	👎 'It was too slow.'	👎 'It was boring.'

Look at the chart above and write about the children's opinions, like this:

1. *The Sound of Music* ..... Jessica, Sushi and Ben liked it, but William didn't like it because it was too slow.

2. *The Wizard of Oz* ....

3. *Star Wars* ....

4. *The Black Stallion* ....

9. Crossword

Across

1. Not fast
3. Something to put your sports things in
4. Paul Roberts
5. A present from the garden for Mother's Day
9. Would you . . . to come?
10. Not man
12. Come . . . 5 o'clock.
13. Something you write with
14. Bread and . . .
15. He's in France . . . the end of May.
17. A flower
18. You can buy it in the Duty Free Shop

Down

1. A month of the year
2. All right
3. You read this
5. I live in a . . . .
6. Not a lot
7. You and I
8. Something warm to wear
11. I start . . . Monday.
16. The music is very . . . .

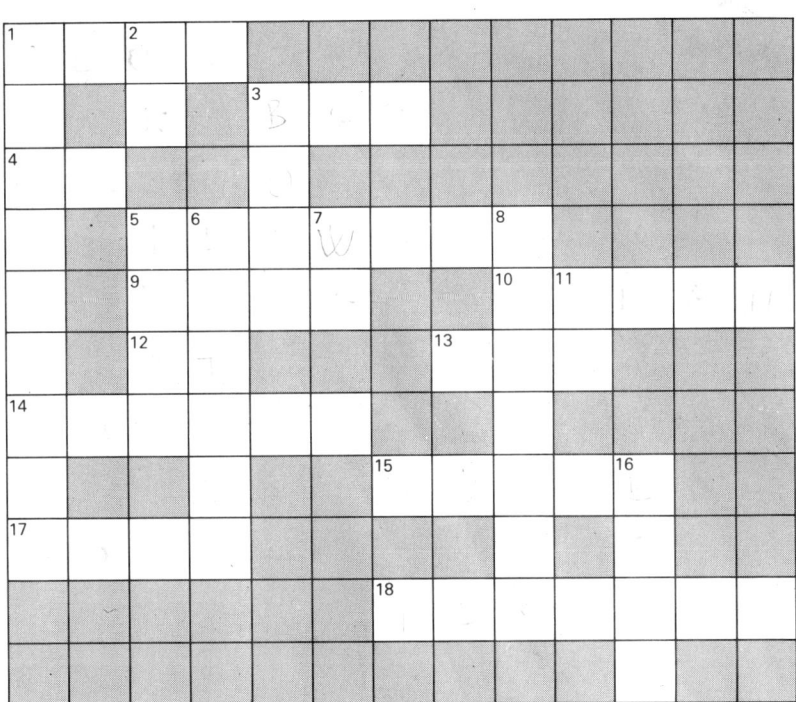

Unit 10

1. Read the text and write in the names of the places and shops on the sketch map of the village below.

Stratton-on-Wye is a small village with four main streets. They are called North Street, South Street, East Street and West Street. The village has a bank, a post office, a Pizza House, a pub called The Queen's Head, a cinema, a café, a record shop and a small flower shop. The bank, a Lloyds bank, is opposite the post office on West Street. The post office is next to the flower shop. The flower shop is on the corner of West Street and North Street. The Pizza House is in North Street next to the cinema. If you walk up North Street it is on your left after the cinema. The cinema is opposite the record shop. On the left of the record shop, on the corner of North Street and East Street is a café. The Queen's Head is opposite the café on the corner of East Street and South Street.

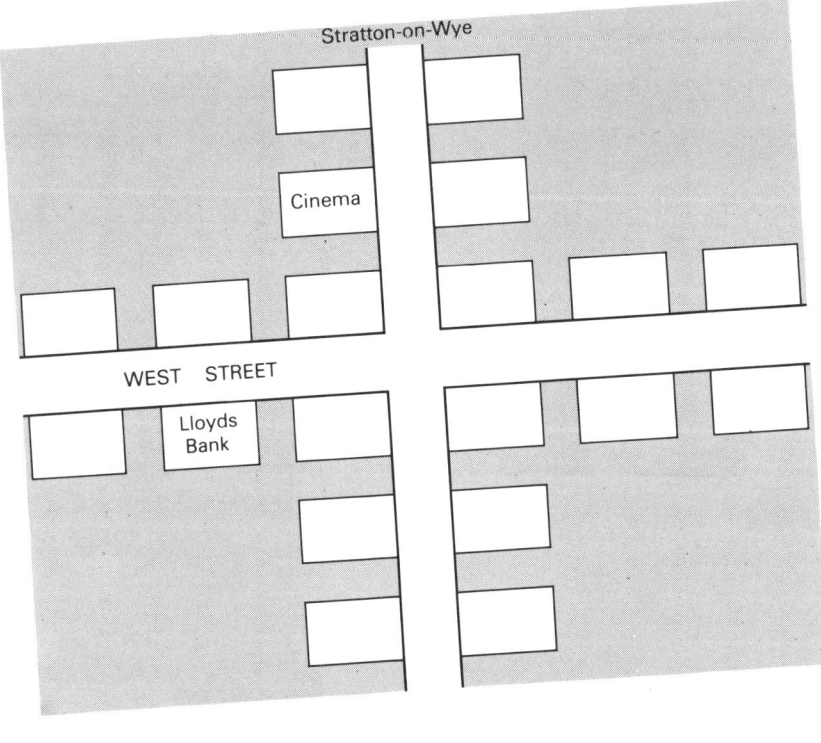

UNIT 10

2. Complete the questionnaire.

STRATEGIES
WANTS TO KNOW ABOUT YOU

We would like to know who you are, what you do in your spare time and what you like and dislike. Please help us and fill in this questionnaire. All the questions are simple and easy to follow. All the answers are in confidence so don't put your name and address. Thank you for your time.

LEISURE RESEARCH QUESTIONNAIRE

1. **About daily newspapers**
   Which daily newspaper/s do you read most often?

2. **About weekly and monthly magazines**
   Which weekly or monthly magazines do you read most often?

3. **About the cinema**
   How often do you go to the cinema?

Twice a week or more?	
Once a week?	
Once a fortnight?	
Once a month?	
Less often?	
Never?	

4. **About the theatre**
   How often do you go to the theatre?

Once a month or more?	
Up to six times a year?	
Once a year?	
Less often?	
Never?	

5. **About classical music**
   How often do you listen to live classical music?

Once a week or more?	
Once a fortnight?	
Once a month?	
Twice a year?	
Less often?	
Never?	

6. **About live non-classical music**
   How often do you listen to live non-classical music (i.e. rock, folk, jazz, funk, reggae, pop, etc.)?

Once a week or more?	
Once a fortnight?	
Once a month?	
Two or three times a year?	
Less often?	
Never?	

UNIT 10

7. About eating in restaurants
How often do you eat out in restaurants of any kind?

5 times a week?	
3 or 4 times a week?	
2 or 3 times a week?	
Once a week?	
Less than once a week but more than once a month?	
Less often?	
Never?	

8. About buying and reading books, including paperbacks
How many books do you buy a month?

4 or more?	
Between 2 and 4?	
Between 1 and 2?	
Less than 1?	
None?	

9. About buying cassettes or records
How many cassettes or records do you buy a month?

4 or more?	
Between 2 and 4?	
Between 1 and 2?	
Less than 1?	
None?	

10. About means of transport
How do you usually travel to your place of work or study?

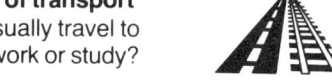

By car?	
By bus?	
By train?	
By underground?	
By tram?	
Other?	

11. About other free time activities
How many times a month do you go to each of the following?

	An art gallery	A disco	A museum	A football match	Roller skating	Other sports	A political meeting	A community activity	An educational activity other than school or college (e.g. an art class)	A physical activity (e.g. a class on Jazz dancing)
4 or more times?										
2 or 3 times?										
Once?										
Less than once?										
Never?										

In your notebook write ten sentences about your spare time and your likes and dislikes.

Unit 11

1. Use the entries in the diary to complete the conversations.

1. Can you come to the cinema with me on Monday evening?

   No, I'm afraid I can't. I'm going to bed early.

2. Would you like to come to tea on Tuesday?

   ....

3. Would you like to go out on Wednesday evening?

   ....

4. What about lunch on Thursday?

   ....

5. Can you come to town with me on Saturday morning then?

   ....

2. Look at the following advertisement for a holiday and complete the conversation.

TRIMAST TRAVEL CHRISTMAS BREAK

Why not join us on 4th December (late) departing Gatwick for our one week pre-Christmas party in a luxury hotel, Palma, Majorca? | Price includes single room, half board, cocktail parties and full entertainments programme. Only £165.

**Contact Trimast Travel, Trimast House, Bournemouth
Phone: 0706 829255**

HELEN: Carol, I'm having a party on December the 4th. Would you like to come?

CAROL: No, I'm afraid *I can't. I'm going on holiday to Majorca.*

HELEN: To Majorca? How long ....? (stay)

CAROL: For a week.

HELEN: How lovely! Where ....? (stay)

CAROL: In a hotel in Palma.

HELEN: Which airport ....? (leave from)

CAROL: From Gatwick.

HELEN: How ....? (get)

CAROL: By train from Victoria. Anyway, have a nice party!

53

UNIT 11

3. Write two questions for each of the following situations. Use the present continuous form of the verb each time.

1. A friend is changing his/her job.

Why ...... *are you changing your job?* ......

When .... ?

2. Some friends are going on holiday.

Where .... ?

How long .... ?

3. Some friends want you to babysit one evening.

Where .... ?

When .... ?

4. Label these clothes.

£26.50

£15.45

£29.95

£39.95

£29.95

£17.99

£45.75

£55.00

£26.50

£24.99

5. Look at the clothes in Exercise 4. Ask to try them on.

1. *Can I try this jacket on, please?*
2. *Can I try these jeans on, please?*
3. ....
4. ....
5. ....
6. ....
7. ....
8. ....

UNIT 11

6. Look at the clothes again. Make conversations like this:

1. A: What a lovely jacket! Can I try it on please?
   B: Yes, certainly.
   A: It's very smart. How much does it cost?
   B: Thirty-nine pounds ninety-five pence.
   A: I think I'll have it.

2. A: .... shoes! .... ?
   B: ....
   A: ....
   B: ....
   A: ....

3. A: .... sweater! .... ?
   B: ....
   A: ....
   B: ....
   A: ....

4. A: .... trousers! .... ?
   B: ....
   A: ....
   B: ....
   A: ....

7. Fill in the missing words. Choose from the verbs in the box. Use the right form of the verb.

come go bring take

1. Would you like to **come** home with me after the class?
2. Let's .... swimming tomorrow afternoon.
3. If you come, please .... your children with you.
4. .... away!
5. Can you .... this book back to the library, please?
6. When are you .... on holiday?
7. Are you .... your mother with you to Spain?
8. Please .... to lunch on Sunday. And .... your holiday photographs with you. I'd love to see them.

FLIGHT INSURANCE & TRAVEL SERVICES LTD

HEAD OFFICE:
12-14 WILLIAM STREET
LONDON W1V 1CD
PHONE: 01-734 7734
TELEX: 268079
CABLES: HENTRAV LONDON W1

27 COPTHALL ROAD
LONDON EC2R 7PB
PHONE: 01-606 7994
TELEX: 268079
CABLES: HENTRAV LONDON EC2

```
                 ITINERARY
FRI 27 MAY
LONDON-STOCKHOLM   FLIGHT SK 526 CONFIRMED
                   ECONOMY CLASS
REPORT 1045 Hrs    LATEST
DEPART 1145 Hrs    LONDON HEATHROW TERMINAL TWO
ARRIVE 1505 Hrs    STOCKHOLM ARLANDA AIRPORT

FRI 27 MAY
One Single Room with Bath Confirmed at:-
Globe Hotel,
Tegelbacken 8,
PO Box 1,056,
S-10123 Stockholm,     Phone (08) 14 26 44
Sweden.                Telex (854) 18890

TUE 31 MAY
STOCKHOLM-LONDON   FLIGHT SK 527 CONFIRMED
                   ECONOMY CLASS
REPORT 1500 Hrs    LATEST
DEPART 1600 Hrs    STOCKHOLM ARLANDA AIRPORT
ARRIVE 1730 Hrs    LONDON HEATHROW TERMINAL TWO

Timings shown are local. ALL BAGGAGE must be
labelled, for allowance see ticket. We advise
that ONWARD/RETURN flights and CHECK IN times
are reconfirmed 72 hrs ahead.
```

8. Here is your itinerary for a trip to Stockholm, Sweden. Use the information to write a short letter (in your notebook) to Ulla Andersson, a Swedish friend. Say when you are arriving and where you are staying. Give the name, address and telephone number of the hotel. Also say how long you are staying in Sweden. End your letter with:

Looking forward to seeing you on Friday, May 27th.

With best wishes.

(*your name*)

Unit 12

1. What do the signs mean?

1. Don't smoke here. ....or...... You mustn't smoke here.
2. ....
3. ....
4. ....
5. ....

2. Match the road sign with the instruction.

A 1. Be careful. There's a roundabout ahead.

B 2. Be careful here. The road turns right.

C 3. Be careful here. There's a crossroad ahead.

D 4. There is a sharp bend in the road. You must turn left.

E 5. You must drive more slowly now.

F 6. You must stop in 100 yards.

G 7. You must stop at the end of this road. There's a T-junction ahead.

UNIT 12

3. Write the correct form of the verb tense in the table below.

PRESENT	PAST
sit	
talk	
	had
give	
	came
	did
go	
take	
watch	
	drove
	dropped
get	

4. Which is correct, a, b or c?

1. A: Did you have a nice weekend?
   B: a) Yes, I had lunch.
   　　b) Yes, I had a cold.
   　　ⓒ) Yes, I did.

2. A: a) What did you do?
   　　b) What do you do?
   　　c) What does he do?

3. B: a) I did go to Cambridge for the day.
   　　b) I went to Cambridge for the day.
   　　c) I go to Cambridge.

4. A: a) Did you have lunch there?
   　　b) Do you have lunch there?
   　　c) Do you enjoy it?

5. B: a) At 1 p.m.
   　　b) Yes, to an Italian restaurant.
   　　c) Yes, at an Italian restaurant.

6. A: a) It's nice.
   　　b) How nice!
   　　c) What nice times!

5. Insert the missing prepositions.
Choose from:

| in | at | with | by | for | to | on | of |

Last summer we went ...**to**... Austria .... our holiday. We travelled .... car and stayed .... relatives on the way. It took us about two days to drive there altogether.

We had a marvellous time. One day we went .... a boat trip. That was great. But I didn't enjoy the camping much. It was quite cold .... the evenings. After a few days, we decided to stay .... a hotel .... the rest .... the holiday. We stayed .... two weeks altogether.

6. Now write questions like this:

1. Ask where they went last summer.   *Where did you go last summer?*
2. Ask how they travelled.
3. Ask where they stayed on the way.
4. Ask how long the journey took.
5. Ask if they did anything special.
6. Ask if they enjoyed the camping.
7. Ask where they stayed after camping.
8. Ask how long they stayed in Austria.

UNIT 12

7. Read this telephone conversation.

ASHA: You are coming to Bristol this weekend, aren't you?
SALLY: Yes, of course.
ASHA: How are you travelling?
SALLY: By train. I'll come after work on Friday evening.
ASHA: Fine. Listen, when you get to Bristol, take a taxi to the flat. Taxis are quite cheap in Bristol.
SALLY: OK.
ASHA: Then we can have supper when you arrive.
SALLY: Great! Have you any plans for the rest of the evening? I'm a bit tired actually.
ASHA: No. I thought we could just sit and talk and perhaps watch the late night film on television before we go to bed.
SALLY: Lovely! I'm looking forward to it. See you then.

Answer these questions.

1. Where is Sally going this weekend? ....

2. How is she travelling? ....

Now read about the weekend. Fill in the missing words.

Last weekend, Sally ..**went**.. to see an old friend from school called Asha.

She .... by train after work on Friday. When she .... to Bristol,

she .... a taxi to Asha's flat. When she .... they ....

supper and then .... and .... for the rest of the evening. They ....

the late night film on television before they .... to bed. They both enjoyed

the evening very much.

Unit 13

1. Write conversations like this:

Two women are working in a noisy factory. They are talking about their weekend.

A: Did you have a nice weekend?
B: What?
A: I said did you have a nice weekend?
B: Oh! No, I didn't.
A: What?
B: I said I didn't have a nice weekend.
A: Oh!
B: Did you?
A: Yes, I did.
B: What?
A: I said I had a nice weekend.
B: Ah!

1. A: Did you see your family at the weekend?

    B: ………………………………………………………………………

    A: I said ………………………………………………………………

    B: ………………………………………………………………………

    A: ………………………………………………………………………

    B: I said ………………………………………………………………

    A: ………………………………………………………………………

    B: ………………………………………………………………………

    A: ………………………………………………………………………

    B: ………………………………………………………………………

    A: I said ………………………………………………………………

    B: Ah!

2. A: Did you go into town on Sunday?

    B: ………………………………………………………………………

    A: I said ………………………………………………………………

    B: ………………………………………………………………………

    A: ………………………………………………………………………

    B: I said ………………………………………………………………

UNIT 13

A: ....
B: ....
A: ....
B: ....
A: I said ....
B: Ah! ....

How young people spent their money last year.

These figures are for the 11-17 age group

	£ million
Comics, magazines, newspapers	50
Make-up	50
Sport	54
Cinema	71
Dancing, discos	81
Eating out	89
Fares	110
Records and tapes	146
Crisps, ice cream, sweets	305
Clothes	315
Savings	380
Total	£1651 million

2. Answer these questions. Write the answers in full.

1. What did the young people spend most of their money on?

   They spent most of their money on clothes.

2. What sort of 'food' did they spend at lot of their money on?

   ....

3. What sort of reading matter did they spend their money on?

   ....

4. How much did they spend on travelling (fares)?

   ....

5. How much did they spend on make-up?

   ....

UNIT 13

3. Look at Doug's diary for yesterday. Write what he did. Use these verbs: meet, go to, watch, have, play.

Diary — MONDAY MAY 22
- A.M. Meet representative from NBC at Heathrow Airport – 8 a.m.
- 11 a.m. – meeting
- LUNCH 12.30 p.m. – lunch with Mr Shore at Mancey's Restaurant
- P.M. 2 p.m. – squash with Mark
- Watch the new film from Focus
- EVENING Theatre – 8 p.m.

1. At 8 a.m. he met a representative from NBC.
2. ....
3. ....
4. ....
5. After squash,
6. ....

4. Make questions and answers like this:

1. How often/eat out?   A: How often do you eat out?
   2/month   B: About twice a month.
   Last week?   A: Did you eat out last week?
   No   B: No, I didn't.

2. How often/buy records?   A:
   2/year   B:
   Last month?   A:
   Yes   B:

3. How often/go dancing?   A:
   3/year   B:
   Last month?   A:
   Yes   B:

4. How often/buy magazines?   A:
   1/month   B:
   Last week?   A:
   No   B:

5. Complete the conversation. Julian is talking to Jane about his holiday. Jane is trying to read a book.

JULIAN: We're going to Portugal next week.
JANE: ...Are you?...

JULIAN: Yes, we're driving there.
JANE: ....

JULIAN: Mm. We always go there for Christmas.
JANE: ....

JULIAN: We've got relatives there.
JANE: ....

JULIAN: They live in Lisbon.
JANE: ....

JULIAN: Yes, it's my sister, in fact.
JANE: ....

JULIAN: Last year we went by boat.
JANE: ....

JULIAN: Yes, but my wife was sick on the trip.
JANE: ....

JULIAN: She doesn't like boat trips at all.
JANE: ....

JULIAN: No. Do you?
JANE: What? Oh sorry! I wasn't listening. Did you say you were going to Spain next week?

6. Make negative questions and answer them.

1. Are you English? Aren't you English?
   That's right. I am.

2. Is this my book? ....

UNIT 13

3. Was he from Manchester? ....
....

4. Were you at Sam's restaurant last night? ....
....

5. Do you like your tea with lemon? ....
....

6. Did they go out last night? ....
....

7. Look at the table and make six requests.

| Can you | ask
tell | the milkman
your children
the woman in the shop
the teacher
your dog
your husband | to
not to | pick the apples off our tree?
give me a size 12?
explain the exercise again?
leave the milk in the sun?
park his car in front of my garage?
eat my slippers? |

1. *Can you ask the milkman not to leave the milk in the sun?*
2. ....
3. ....
4. ....
5. ....
6. ....

Write out the requests again, using him, her, it **or** them.

7. *Can you ask him not to leave the milk in the sun?*
8. ....
9. ....
10. ....
11. ....
12. ....

8.

Camp Blackwater is a summer camp for young people of different nationalities between the ages of 13 and 17. It's in New Jersey in the United States. The camp members are planning a barbecue. Joe, the social organiser, goes up to the camp leader, Jenny, with a list of things which he wants the camp members to do.

Barbeque Evening
8.30 p.m. Saturday

Must:
- learn the words of 'My Bonnie' and 'She'll be coming round the mountain'
- be ready to sing a national song
- collect some money to buy some food
- bring a guitar if they have one

Mustn't:
- be late
- bring transistor radios or cassette recorders with them
- bring any alcohol with them

Write Joe's requests to Jenny.

1. Can you ask them to learn the words of 'My Bonnie' and 'She'll be coming round the mountain'?
2. ......
3. ......
4. ......
5. ......
6. ......
7. ......

Unit 14

1. Rewrite these sentences.

1. Those are my shoes.   Those are mine.
2. That's our house.   ....
3. Those are her boots.   ....
4. This is their car.   ....
5. Those are your books.   ....
6. Those are his photographs.   ....
7. That's her jacket.   ....

2. Ask and answer like this:

1. hat/me   Whose hat is this? It's mine.
2. tie/John   Whose tie is this? It's John's.
3. glasses/us   ....
4. bag/Martha   ....
5. shorts/my sister   ....
6. bicycle/David   ....
7. tape recorder/them   ....

3. Make statements and questions like this:

1. my pen/yours   This is my pen. Which one is yours?
2. John's boots/hers   These are John's boots. Which are hers?
3. Sally's car/ours   ....
4. our records/theirs   ....
5. their cassettes/yours   ....
6. his book/hers   ....
7. Mr Barton's room/Miss Harman's   ....
8. Susan's running shoes/Bill's.   ....

UNIT 14

4. Punctuate this letter. Put commas, full stops, question marks, exclamation marks (!) and apostrophes where necessary.

Dear Jojo,

Thank you for your letter. It was good to hear from you. What awful news about your accident! I hope you get better soon.

Last Sunday Paul and I went to see Cats. It's a musical. It was really fantastic. We both enjoyed it very much. I'm enjoying London so much, perhaps I'll stay here a bit longer.

The conference is finished now. Our film was quite successful, but Paul and Diana's won first prize. I must go now. Look after yourself and write again soon.

Love,
Joanne

5. Which is correct, a, b or c?

1. A: Your English is good!

   B: a) Well, I'm studying English for six years.
   b) Well, I've studied English for six years.
   c) Well, I study English for six years.

2. A: How long have you lived here?

   B: a) For two years.
   b) For two year.
   c) In two years.

3. a) Can you have breakfast yet?
   b) Have you had breakfast yet?
   c) Do you have breakfast yet?

4. A: Whose is this hat?

   B: a) It's Jack.
      b) This is my hat.
      c) It's mine.

5. This isn't my pen.   a) Whose is it?
                        b) Who's is it?
                        c) Who is it?

6. I like the red shoes.   a) Which one do *you* like?
                           b) Which ones do *you* like?
                           c) Which red one do *you* like?

6. Look at the pictures and make conversations.

1. shorts
   stripes/stars

2. calendar
   Marilyn Monroe/a cat

3. glasses
   tall with flowers/short with fruit

4. lunchbox
   Bumble/Fantastic Fred

1. A: Which shorts do you like?
   B: I like the ones with stripes on them.

2. A: ....
   B: ....
      ....

3. A: ....
   B: ....
      ....

4. A: ....
   B: ....
      ....

UNIT 14

7. Ask and answer questions like this:

1. Have breakfast/what time A: Have you had breakfast?
 B: Yes, I have.
 A: What time did you have it?
8 a.m. B: I had it at 8 a.m.

2. Have lunch/what A: ......
 B: ......
 A: ......
fish and chips B: ......

3. Make your bed/when A: ......
 B: ......
 A: ......
after breakfast B: ......

4. Play tennis this week/who with A: ......
 B: ......
 A: ......
Mark B: ......

8. Look at Exercise 7 again and write sentences.

1. I've had breakfast.
   I had it at 8 a.m.

2. ......

3. ......

4. ......

Unit 15 | Consolidation

1. Answer these questions about Diana.

1. What is Diana's surname? _Her surname is Trent._
2. Does she live in London? ....
3. Where does she live? ....
4. Is she married? ....
5. Has she got any children? ....
6. Who does she work for? ....
7. What does she do there? ....
8. Why has she come to London? ....
9. Where is she staying? ....
10. What was her film about? ....
11. Did it win a prize? ....
12. Why is she happy at the end of the story? ....

Use this information to write a paragraph about Diana. Start like this:

Diana Trent lives in Manchester. She is ....

UNIT 15

2. And finally YOU.

What is your full name? ....

What nationality are you? ....

What language do you usually speak at home? ....

Where do you live? ....

How long have you lived there? ....

Are you married? ....

Have you got any children? ....

Do you like learning English? ....

Have you ever been to England? ....

Did you like it? ....

How long have you studied English? ....

What did you do last summer? ....

Did you enjoy yourself? ....

What would you like to do next summer? ....

Now write a paragraph about yourself.

Grammar revision

1. Complete the following conversation choosing the correct alternative a, b or c each time.

Bob and Carol have invited a friend of theirs, Tom, to supper. Tom is going to bring a friend, Monique, with him.

(*door bell rings*)

CAROL: Hello, Tom! Nice to see you again!

TOM: (1) a) Hi, Carol! b) How do you do! c) Good evening! Sorry we're a bit late. — *a*

CAROL: (2) a) It's nothing. b) It's fine. c) That's all right. Bob isn't ready yet. (3) a) He cooks. b) He cooked. c) He's cooking in the kitchen. — *c*

TOM: Carol, (4) a) she's Monique. b) this is Monique. c) that's Monique. — *b*

CAROL: Hello, Monique. Do come in.

MONIQUE: Thank you.

CAROL: Are you French?

MONIQUE: (5) a) No, I'm not. b) No, you aren't. c) No, it isn't. I'm Belgian. I'm from Brussels. — *a*

CAROL: Oh, how nice!

MONIQUE: (6) a) Were you ever there? b) Did you go there? c) Have you ever been there? — *b*

CAROL: Yes, Bob and I (7) a) have spent b) did spend c) spent a year there when Bob worked for the EEC. Ah, here's Bob now. — *c*

BOB: Hi, Tom! How are you?

TOM: (8) a) I am well. b) OK, thanks. c) Very good, thank you. — *c*

CAROL: Bob, this is Monique. She's from Belgium.

BOB: Hello, Monique. Can you speak some English?

MONIQUE: (9) a) Yes, I can little. b) I am speaking a little. c) Yes, I can a little. — *c*

TOM: She can speak it very well.

CAROL: Good. Now, what about something to drink. (10) a) What would you like? b) What do you like? c) What will you want? — *b*

BOB: (11) a) What is it? b) What is there? c) Which do you have? — *b*

CAROL: I've got lager, wine, sherry, juice.... Monique?

MONIQUE: (12) a) I like b) I like to have c) I'd like a glass of orange juice, please. — *c*

TOM: Can I have a lager, Carol?

BOB: And one for me, too, please. Now, I must go back to the kitchen. I'm making supper.

CAROL: (13) a) I want to sit b) Let's sit c) Why not sit in the garden. — *c*

BOB: That's a good idea. (14) a) Are there b) Are they c) Is there any chairs out there? — *a*

CAROL: Yes, there are. (15) a) I have taken b) I did take c) I took some out into the garden at lunchtime.

TOM: (16) a) Is it a beautiful evening? b) It isn't a beautiful evening. c) Isn't it a beautiful evening? — *c*

CAROL: Yes, it's lovely. I think (17) a) we have b) we're going to have c) we will have a nice, hot summer. — *a*

(*dog barks*)

CAROL: Hello, Benjie. This is our dog, Benjamin. (18) a) Do you like b) Are you going to like c) You will like dogs, Monique? — *a*

MONIQUE: (19) a) Yes, I am. b) Yes, I do. c) No, I don't like it. — *b*

CAROL: Oh good. Benjamin's a very old dog, aren't you, Benjamin?

MONIQUE: (20) a) How old was he? b) What is the age? c) How old is he? — *c*

CAROL: He's fourteen! Have you got any animals at home?

MONIQUE: (21) a) Yes, we get b) Yes, we've got c) Yes, we're having three cats and two dogs. We live in the country. — *b*

73

TOM: (22) a) What are you doing now, Carol? b) What you do now, Carol? c) What is your work now, Carol?

CAROL: Oh, I'm still working for UNICEF. It's interesting but the money (23) a) aren't b) wasn't c) isn't very good. What about you? (24) a) Will you find a job now? b) Have you found a job yet? c) Are you finding a job now?

TOM: No, not yet. I'm still looking, unfortunately.

CAROL: What about you, Monique? (25) a) What are you doing? b) What do you do? c) What is your work?

MONIQUE: I'm a translater (26) a) by b) on c) for an internatonal pharmaceutical company.

CAROL: That sounds interesting. How long (27) a) are you working there b) did you work there c) have you worked there?

MONIQUE: For six months. I enjoy (28) a) working b) to work c) my working there very much.

TOM: By the way, Monique, (29) a) have you seen b) did you see c) did you saw the programme on TV last night about interpreters' jobs with the United Nations?

MONIQUE: Yes, I did. It was quite good. I'd like a job there!

BOB: Come on, everyone. Food's ready. I hope (30) a) you would like it. b) you are liking it. c) you like it. It's barbecued spare ribs and baked potatoes in their jackets.

TOM: It sounds great. I'm starving!

2. Write the missing parts in the spaces provided.

infinitive	past	past participle
be	was	been
buy		
	came	
		done
find		
	got	
		given
go		
	had	
		known
like		
	lost	
		made
play		
	read	
		said
send		
	saw	
		sat
speak		
	stole	
		taken
tell		
	thought	
		worn
write		

3. Complete the following sentences. Choose between the present simple tense (I work) **and the present continuous** (I am working) **of the verbs in brackets.**

1. My sister usually (have) only a cup of coffee for breakfast.

   ....
   ....

2. Look out of the window! At last the sun (shine)!

   ....
   ....

3. Both my parents (work) full-time. They (be) never home before six in the evening.

   ....
   ....

4. Oh good! The postman (come). I hope there's a letter for me.

   ....
   ....

5. My girlfriend's a student nurse and she (not like) working at night at all!

   ....
   ....

6. I know someone who (live) in London and (work) in Edinburgh. He (fly) to work every day.

   ....
   ....

7. I'm afraid my mother is out. She (visit) her sister in hospital. Can I take a message?

   ....
   ....

4. Complete the following conversations. Choose between the past simple tense (I worked) **and the present perfect** (I have worked) **of the verbs in brackets.**

1. A: I (go) to the dentist last week and I (have) three fillings.

   ....

   ....

   B: Really? I (not see) the dentist for two years!

   ....

   ....

2. A: I'm hungry. (Have) you anything to eat yet?

   ....

   ....

   B: Yes, I (go) to the canteen for lunch at 12.30.

   ....

   ....

3. A: You're new here, aren't you?

   ....

   ....

   B: No, we (live) here for four years!

   ....

   ....

4. A: How do you like the house?

   ....

   ....

   B: It's great! We (rent) a one-roomed flat last year so this is like a palace!

   ....

   ....

5. Look at the following sentences. Mark the boxes with a tick (✓) if they are correct and with a cross (×) if they are wrong. If they are wrong, write the correct sentence in the space provided below.

1. We arrived to England in September. ✗
2. Can I try these shoes on, please? ✓
3. I want that she buys some sweets. ☐
4. I sent the letter in august the 4st. ☐
5. Did you enjoy the film? ✓
6. Do you like some more salad? ☐
7. Please don't talk so loudly. ☐
8. She's a friend of me. ☐

We arrived in England in september

I want her to buy some sweets.

I sent the letter on Aug the fourth 4th

Would you like some more salad?

Please don't talk so loud.

{ She's my friend
{ She's a friend of mine

6. Complete the word pairs.

bread and *butter* ....

table and ....

pen and ....

mother and ....

brother and ....

husband and ....

son and ....

Saturday and ....

up and ....

day and ....

town and ....

black and ....

hungry and *thirsty* ....

food and ....

north and ....

young and ....